First Facts®

Snakes

Copperheads

by Joanne Mattern

Consultant:
Robert T. Mason, PhD
Professor of Zoology
J.C. Braly Curator of Vertebrates
Oregon State University, Corvallis

Capstone
press®

Mankato, Minnesota

First Facts is published by Capstone Press,
151 Good Counsel Drive, P.O. Box 669, Mankato, Minnesota 56002.
www.capstonepress.com

Library of Congress Cataloging-in-Publication Data
Mattern, Joanne, 1963–
    Copperheads / by Joanne Mattern.
    p. cm. — (First facts. Snakes)
    Includes bibliographical references and index.
    Summary: "A brief introduction to copperheads, including their habitat, food, and
life cycle" — Provided by publisher.
    ISBN-13: 978-1-4296-1925-7 (hardcover)
    ISBN-10: 1-4296-1925-2 (hardcover)
    1. Copperhead — Juvenile literature. I. Title.
QL666.O69M35 2009
597.96'3 — dc22   2007051905

Editorial Credits
Lori Shores, editor; Ted Williams, designer and illustrator; Danielle Ceminsky,
    illustrator; Jo Miller, photo researcher

Photo Credits
© 2008 Jupiterimages Corporation, cover
Alamy/Papilio, 1
Bruce Coleman Inc./Joe McDonald, 13, 14–15, 21
Dreamstime/Rdodson, 10–11
Getty Images Inc./National Geographic/George Grall, 20
Pete Carmichael, 16
Shutterstock/Nahimoff, background texture (throughout)
UNICORN Stock Photos/Jack Milchanowski, 7, 8–9
Visuals Unlimited/Jack Milchanowski, 12; Jim Merli, 18; Joe McDonald, 5

Essential content terms are **bold** and are defined on the bottom of the page where they first appear.

1 2 3 4 5 6 13 12 11 10 09 08

Table of Contents

Meet the Copperhead

Watch your step walking through the woods. You just might step on a copperhead snake! Sometimes it's hard to see a copperhead on the ground. But it's easy to see how this **reptile** got its name. This snake's head is red-brown, or the color of copper.

Fun Fact!
Lizards, turtles, alligators, and crocodiles are reptiles too.

reptile: a cold-blooded animal that breathes air and has a backbone

A Woodland Home

Copperheads live in many parts of the eastern United States. They live in woods and rocky places. They can often be found near bodies of water.

Copperhead Range

☐ where copperheads live

North America

South America

Europe

Africa

Asia

Australia

Antarctica

N
W — E
S

Snakes are cold-blooded. Their
body temperature changes with the
temperature of the air and ground
around them. Copperheads often lie in
patches of sunlight to warm up.

Long and Scaly

Most copperheads are about 3 feet (1 meter) long. That's as long as a large dog. Some copperheads have grown to be 4.5 feet (1.4 meters) long.

All snakes have **scales** covering their bodies. They might look slimy, but scales are hard and dry. Copperheads shed their scaly skin as they grow.

scales: small pieces of hard skin

Camouflage

Copperheads have brown and copper spots and bands on their bodies. The colors provide great **camouflage**. Copperheads hide in dead leaves and wait for **prey** to come near.

Fun Fact!

Copperheads often hide under leaves. People can be bitten if they step on the snake by mistake.

camouflage: colors that match surroundings
prey: animals hunted for food

Venom, Anyone?

Copperheads have dangerous **venom**. They store their venom in pouches on the sides of their heads.

venom: a harmful liquid

A copperhead has two sharp teeth called fangs. When the copperhead bites, venom flows through the hollow fangs. Copperhead venom is strong enough to kill small animals within just a few minutes.

Fun Fact!
A copperhead's venom is not strong enough to kill an adult. But it can make a person very sick.

A Deadly Bite

A copperhead strikes very fast. Then it waits for its venom to kill the prey. Once the animal is dead, the snake swallows it whole.

Most snakes will eat anything that fits in their mouths. Copperheads usually eat small mammals and frogs. Sometimes they eat smaller snakes.

Fun Fact!
If a copperhead loses a fang, it grows a new one.

venom
pouch

pit

tongue

Sensing Heat

Copperheads belong to a group of snakes called pit vipers. Pit vipers have small holes, or pits, that sense heat. The pits are between their eyes and the tips of their noses. These special organs help copperheads find prey.

Fun Fact!
Snakes use their noses to smell, of course. But they can also "smell" by picking up scents with their forked tongues.

Life Cycle of a Copperhead

Newborn
Two to 20 snakes are born at one time.

Young
Young copperheads eat small lizards and frogs.

Adult
Copperheads are ready to mate in three years.

Young

18

Copperhead Families

Male and female copperheads mate in the spring. Then in the fall, the female copperhead gives birth. Copperhead babies are born alive and ready to hunt.

Newborn copperheads are only about 8 inches (20 centimeters) long. They are lighter in color than adults. Copperheads change colors as they grow.

Fun Fact!
Young copperheads trick prey into coming close by wiggling their tails. Their little yellow tails look like worms.

Staying Safe

Sometimes a copperhead will shake its tail to scare an enemy. When the tail moves quickly against dry leaves, it sounds like a rattlesnake's rattle.

Amazing but True!

Copperheads have a stinky way of defending themselves. They produce a bad-smelling liquid called musk. When threatened, the snake squirts a little musk from a gland near the tail. The odor is so strong that it keeps the enemy away.

Glossary

camouflage (KAM-uh-flahzh) — coloring that makes animals, people, and objects look like their surroundings

prey (PRAY) — an animal hunted by another animal for food

reptile (REP-tile) — a cold-blooded animal that breathes air and has a backbone

scale (SKALE) — one of the small pieces of hard skin that cover the body of a fish, snake, or other reptile

venom (VEN-uhm) — a harmful liquid produced by some animals

Read More

Doeden, Matt. *Copperheads*. World of Reptiles. Mankato, Minn.: Capstone Press, 2005.

Murray, Julie. *Copperheads*. Animal Kingdom. Edina, Minn.: Abdo, 2005.

O'Hare, Ted. *Copperheads*. Amazing Snakes. Vero Beach, Fla.: Rourke, 2005.

Internet Sites

FactHound offers a safe, fun way to find Internet sites related to this book. All of the sites on FactHound have been researched by our staff.

Here's how:
1. Visit *www.facthound.com*
2. Choose your grade level.
3. Type in this book ID **1429619252** for age-appropriate sites. You may also browse subjects by clicking on letters, or by clicking on pictures and words.
4. Click on the **Fetch It** button.

FactHound will fetch the best sites for you!

Index